C.S.I.
BONE DETECTIVES

John Townsend

CLASH

J614. 7

Copyright © ticktock Entertainment Ltd 2008

First published in Great Britain in 2008 by ticktock Media Ltd,
The Old Sawmill, 103 Goods Station Road, Tunbridge Wells, Kent, TN1 2DP

ticktock project editor: Ruth Owen
ticktock project designer: Sara Greasley
ticktock picture researcher: Lizzie Knowles

**With thanks to series editors Honor Head and Jean Coppendale,
and consultant John Cassella, Principal Lecturer in Forensic Science, Staffordshire University, UK**

Thank you to Lorraine Petersen and the members of nasen

ISBN 978 1 84696 711 5 pbk

Printed in China
9 8 7 6 5 4 3 2

A CIP catalogue record for this book is available from the British Library.

Picture credits (t=top; b=bottom; c=centre; l=left; r=right):
Bone Clones, Inc & boneclones.com: 11bl, 11br, 13 all. Robert Destefano/ Alamy: 24. Michael Donne/ Science Photo
Library: 5r, 28, 29. Mauro Fermariello/ Science Photo Library: 6-7, 10, 21, 25. Mehau Kulyk/ Science Photo Library: OFC
Background. Living Art Enterprises, LLC/ Science Photo Library: 26r. Dr P Marazz/ Science Photo library: 26l.
Donald E. Miller: 31. Louise Murray/ Science Photo Library: 9. Philippe Psaila/ Science Photo Library: 12. Science Photo
Library: 14. Shutterstock: 1, 2, 4t, 5l, 8t, 11tr, 15t, 19, 27t, 30. Pasquale Sorrentino/ Science Photo Library: 17. Volker
Steger/ Science Photo Library: 18. Jack Sullivan/ Alamy: 8b. Kaj R. Svensson/ Science Photo Library: 20t, 20b, 27b.
Zephyr/ Science Photo Library: 23.

Every effort has been made to trace copyright holders, and we apologise in advance for any omissions. We would be pleased to
insert the appropriate acknowledgments in any subsequent edition of this publication.

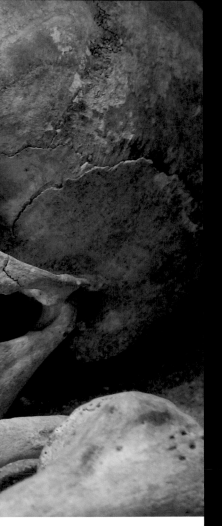

Contents

CHAPTER 1

A GRIM DISCOVERY

A scream fills the forest!

You run through the trees and see someone pointing in horror.

Sticking out of the ground is a human skull. This could be a crime scene.

Call the police...

...don't touch anything!

The police arrive with the crime scene investigators. They are known as CSIs.

The CSIs put on white suits, masks and gloves. The suits and gloves stop the CSIs leaving hairs or fingerprints at the scene.

They start investigating and soon the CSIs find a skeleton.

It's time to call the bone detectives!

Bone detectives are forensic scientists. Their job is to study bones. They can find out the age, height, sex and race of a skeleton.

Bone detectives can find out the medical history of a skeleton. They can even find out how a person died.

CHAPTER 2
THE SKELETON STARTS TO SPEAK

At a crime scene the bone detectives look for clues.

- Are they all human bones?

- Could some be animal bones?

- Are the bones from one human or more?

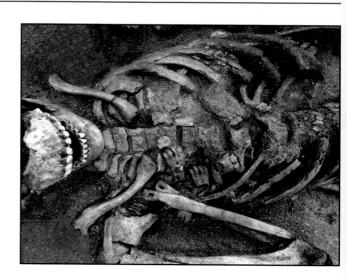

- Is it a whole skeleton?

- How is the skeleton lying? This could give clues to how the person died.

- Was the person killed in an accident?

Could this be a murder case?

Brushing dirt off the bones can show:

- Body tissue (if it hasn't rotted away)
- Hair
- Bits of clothes

Brushing dirt off a bone

A bone detective takes a photograph of all the bones in the forest. Then the bones are taken to the lab.

In the lab a bone detective lays out the whole skeleton. She examines its size and shape.

She can tell by measuring certain bones if it's a male or female. She doesn't need the whole skeleton.

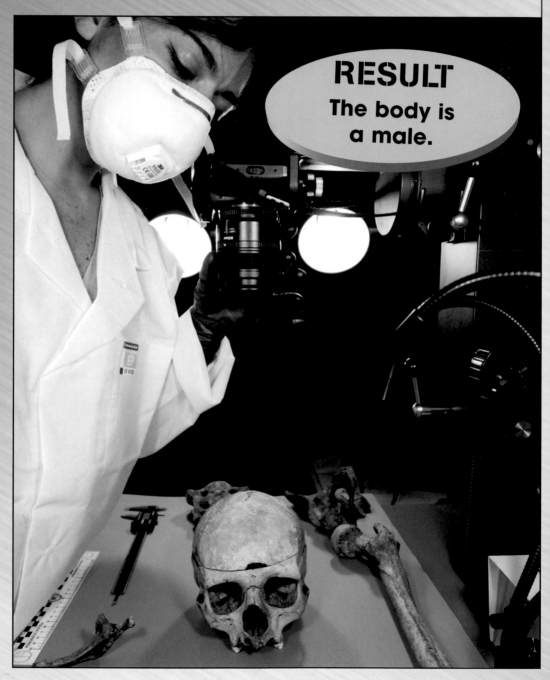

RESULT
The body is a male.

These are the clues the bone detective looks for:

Male   ## Female

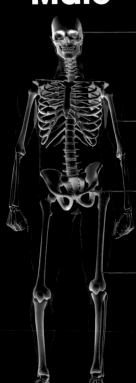

Skull shape

Males have thicker arm bones

Pelvis shape

Size and shape of thigh bones

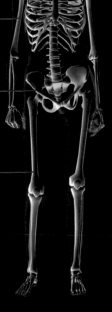

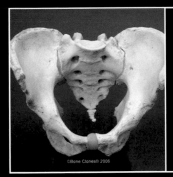

PELVIS SHAPE
A female pelvis has a bigger opening. This is because women give birth to babies.

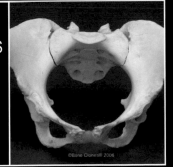

NEED TO KNOW
- The adult human skeleton has 206 bones.
- The height of a person is usually five times longer than the upper arm bone.

Next another bone detective works out the skeleton's age and race.

The skeleton's measurements are compared with other bones that are the average size for different ages.

There are other age clues, too.

Young children have gaps between their bones. All the gaps close up when a person is in their 20s.

A person's skull and nose shape can show their race.

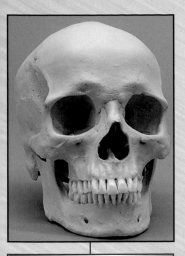

Male European skull

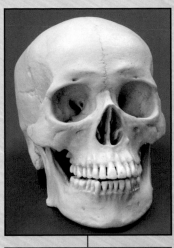

Male Asian skull

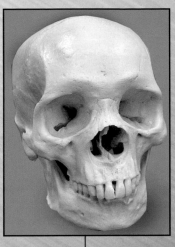

Male African skull

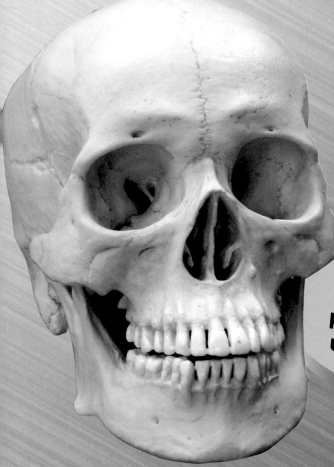

RESULT
The skeleton is probably Asian and under 30 years old.

Bones can show all sorts of personal details about the dead person.

Bones can show how fit and healthy the person was. If the person ate unhealthy food, the bones will lack some minerals.

The skeleton from the forest gives the bone detectives a clue.

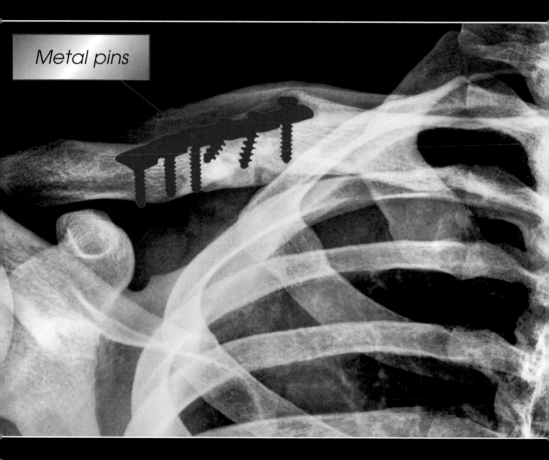

Metal pins

The collar-bone has been broken in the past. It is held together with metal pins. Hospital records can be checked to see who it might be.

By comparing the size and shape of a skeleton's arm bones, the bone detectives can work out if the person was left or right-handed. This shows the victim was right-handed.

He may also have been an active sportsman.

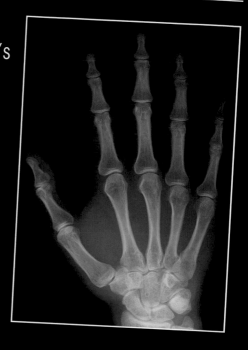

Could this be our skeleton?

CHAPTER 3 LOOKING FOR CLUES

What other clues can the skeleton give us?

There's no flesh left on the bones. In warm weather, flesh can rot away within months.

A bone detective takes a bone sample to test for decay.

The tests show there's been little decay.

RESULT
The victim has not been dead for long.

The police have records of people who are missing. The missing persons records show the names and details of the missing people.

The police can check the records of young men who have gone missing in the past few months. Could one of them be our skeleton?

A DNA test will tell.

Cells in our bones and blood are unique. They contain unique information called DNA.

Bone sample

DNA tests are done on a bone sample from the skeleton.

Special machines read the DNA. They show the information in a pattern called a profile.

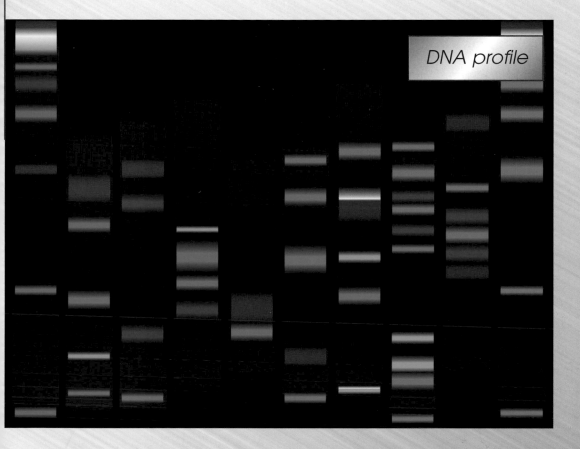

DNA profile

Police computers store millions of DNA profiles. There are profiles of people from all around the world.

DNA from the skeleton may match the DNA profile of a missing person.

NEED TO KNOW

Everyone's DNA is unique except for identical twins!

CHAPTER 4

TEETH TALK

The DNA tests lead nowhere! There is no missing persons record to match. But the skeleton's teeth may hold some clues.

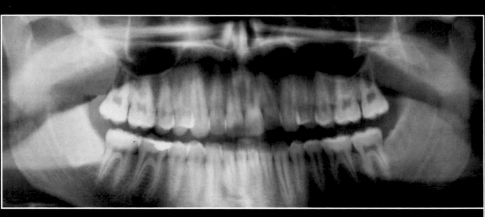

Our skeleton has no wisdom teeth.

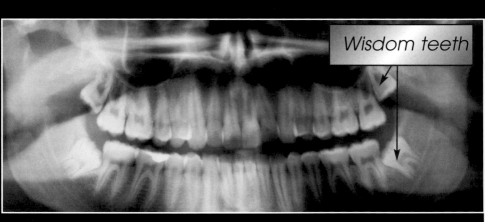

Wisdom teeth

Wisdom teeth grow at the back of the mouth. They have usually grown by the time someone is 18 years old. This means our skeleton was probably under 18.

Next, the skeleton's teeth are photographed. The police show the photographs to dentists in the area where the skeleton was found.

Dentists keep records such as X-rays and moulds of people's teeth. The dentists compare the photographs to their records.

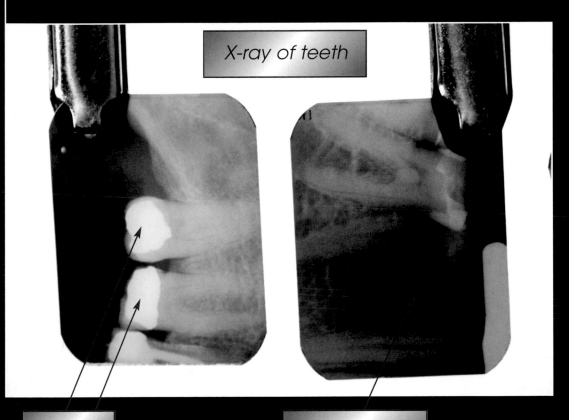

X-ray of teeth

Fillings

Missing tooth

Our skeleton's teeth match a dentist's record!

RESULT
The records identify the victim as Peter Chin.

CHAPTER 5
WAS IT MURDER?

The big question is:

how did Peter Chin die?

There are **FIVE** possible ways:
1. Natural causes – such as old age.
2. An accident.
3. Suicide – you kill yourself.
4. Murder – you are killed by someone.
5. Manslaughter – someone kills you, but it is an accident.

Peter's skull has a fracture. It could mean he was hit with a blunt object. That would be murder.

Or it could mean he fell onto something. That could be an accident.

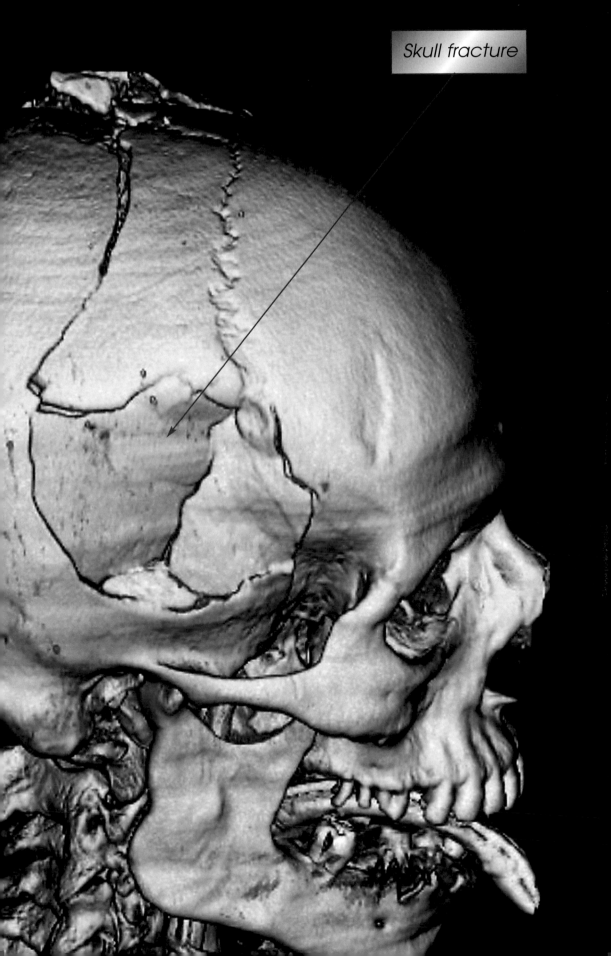

Skull fracture

In a murder case, bone damage can tell a bone detective what weapon was used to kill a person.

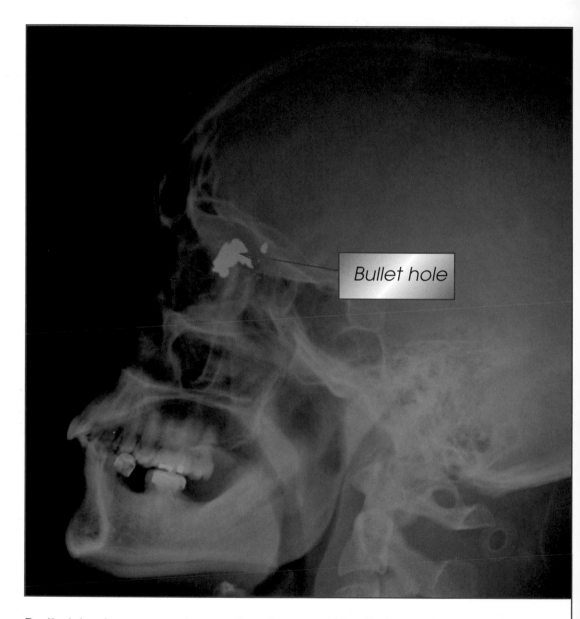

Bullet hole

Bullet holes can show the type of bullet and gun used.

The shape of other holes can show if the weapon was a metal bar, an axe or a bigger object.

This is a piece of human bone with stab marks.
Experts can match a knife to the stab marks.

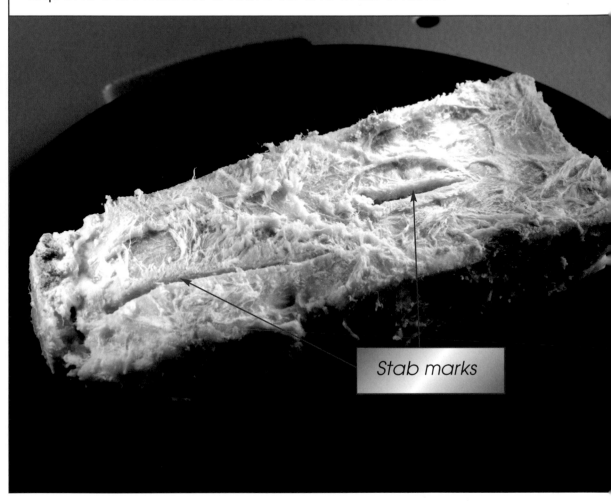

Stab marks

NEED TO KNOW

Marks on wrist or ankle bones could prove a murder victim's hands or feet were tied together.

A bone detective can piece together the puzzle...

...SO WHAT'S PETER'S STORY?

His neck has
a major break.

He also has
ankle fractures.

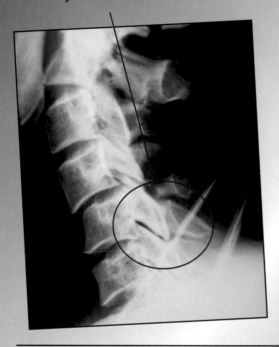

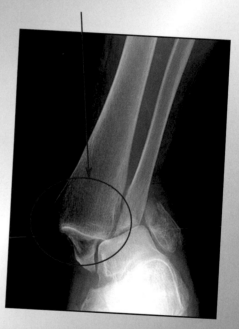

His neck injury suggests a fall from a height.
If someone lands on their feet, the force can
shoot up their legs and spine. This can break
the neck at the base of the skull.

He hit his head as he fell and
fractured his skull.

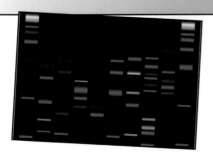

THE RESULTS...

BONE ANALYSIS REPORT

Sex:	male
Age:	16 years
Race:	Asian
Height:	170 cm
Physical details:	good health, right-handed
Cause of death:	broken neck
Other evidence:	broken ankles and neck fracture at base of skull. Plus position of skeleton show victim fell from a tree.
DNA check:	positive
Dental/hospital records:	positive
Identity:	Peter Chin
Year of death:	2008
Verdict:	Accident

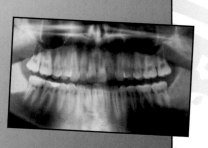

CASE SOLVED!

CHAPTER 6

FITTING THE FACE

Sometimes bone detectives can't solve the puzzle. But forensic scientists can show what a dead person looked like. They use the skull to make a model of the person's face.

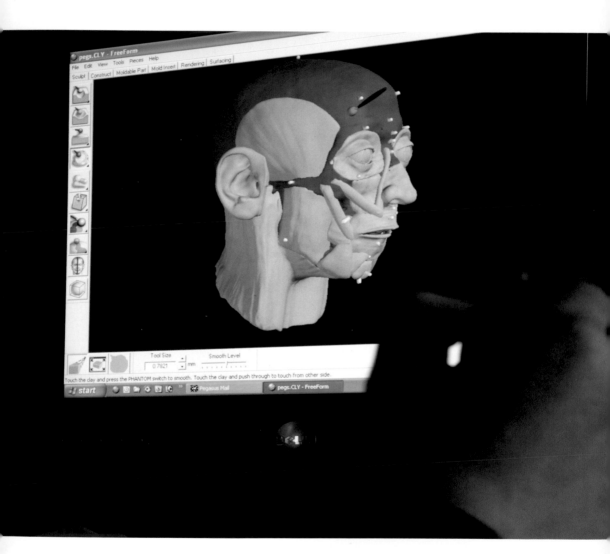

First, the shape of the skull is scanned into a computer and examined.

Layers of muscles made from clay are added.
This builds up the face. False eyes are added.

Finally, the face is painted so it looks real.

Clay muscles

False eyes

The police issue a photograph and ask the public,

"Did you know this person?"

NEED TO KNOW WORDS

bone detective A scientist who studies bones from crime scenes. Bone detectives are also called forensic anthropologists. Sometimes they study ancient bones from historic sites.

crime scene Any place where a crime has happened.

crime scene investigator (CSI) A person who examines a crime scene and collects evidence from it.

decay To rot or break down over time.

DNA The special code in the centre (or nucleus) of each person's cells. Our DNA makes us unique.

evidence Facts and signs that can show what happened during a crime.

forensic Detailed information from a crime. Forensic evidence is used in court cases.

forensic scientist An expert who examines evidence from crime scenes to work out what happened.

fracture A break in a bone.

identity A person's name and details.

race A group of people with the same skin colour, or culture or ancestors.

unique The only one of its kind.

verdict The final decision of what happened.

victim A person who is hurt or killed.

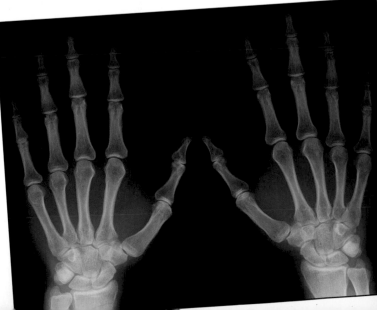

BONE DETECTIVE CASEFILE

Clea Koff is a British/American bone detective. In 1996, Clea went to Rwanda in Africa to work on her biggest case.

During 1994, half a million people were killed in Rwanda in a war between two tribes.

At one mass grave, Clea and other bone detectives dug up

493 bodies. They examined the bodies. They were able to work out that most of the people had been killed by blows from clubs and large knives. They also worked out that about 75% of the skeletons were women, and 25% were children.

Clea's evidence showed that the bodies were women and children who could not defend themselves. They were not the bodies of soldiers fighting each other in a war. Important people had ordered the killings of the women and children. Clea's evidence helped to prove these people were guilty of this crime.

BONES AND CRIME ONLINE

Websites
http://www.pbs.org/opb/historydetectives/techniques/forensic_feature.html
See what different bones in a skeleton can reveal

http://www.sciencenewsforkids.org/articles/20041215/Feature1.asp
All about the crime lab, including bone detection

http://science.howstuffworks.com/csi.htm
All about the world of CSI

31

Index